KU-628-445

Vedic Maths

....

Simplified Vedic Techniques for Multiplication, Division, Squaring and Cubing

....

Himanshu Pancholi

A Wilco Book

Outstanding works of universal interest

© 2014 *Wilco* Publishing House

ISBN: 9788182528895

VEDIC MATHS
Himanshu Pancholi

This edition published in 2020 by
Wilco International, Mumbai - India
Tel: (91-22) 2204 1420 / 2284 2574
E-mail: wilco@wilcobooks.com
Website: wilcobooks.com
        wilcopicturelibrary.com

Printed and bound in India by Thomson press India Ltd.

All rights reserved. This publication may not be reproduced, stored in a retrieval system or transmitted in any form or by any means, electronic, mechanical, photocopying, recording or otherwise, without the prior permission of the publishers.

DEDICATED TO...

I dedicate this book to my respectable parents, my sweet little sister and my lovely wife.....

ACKNOWLEDGEMENTS

I express my sincere gratitude to all those who have helped me publish this book. Hereby, I want to thank my parents, my sister and my wife who supported me throughout the making of this book.

I sincerely thank all my friends who have always been around and provided their help and advice.

I also express my sincere thanks to Mr. Jaisukh Shah, Proprietor of Wilco Publishing House, Mumbai for publishing this book with valuable suggestions to make it better.

The feedback on this book, if you wish, may please be sent to the Publisher's attention at wilco@wilcobooks.com

CONTENTS

INTRODUCTION

Vedic Mathematics is a unique collection of techniques which helps to solve any arithmetical problem in an extremely short duration of time with a high degree of accuracy.

Vedic Mathematics is said to have been rediscovered from the Vedas between 1911 and 1918 by Swami Bharati Krishna Tirtha. It consists of 16 *Sutras*, which are also called Word-formulae or Aphorisms. Any arithmetical problem can be solved mentally with the help of these *Sutras*.

This book mainly focuses on basic arithmetical problems such as multiplication, division, squares and cubes. Vedic Mathematics will change your outlook towards modern mathematics and help you develop a keen interest in various problem solving techniques. In this book, every chapter starts with simple problems and as it progresses, problems become difficult. Exercises provided at the end of each chapter will help you to apply the techniques.

This book is highly recommended for students appearing for entrance exams like CAT, CET, etc. Apart from this, corporate professionals can make use of this book in their day to day life. After a certain time, you will prefer to use your brain over the calculator. This book will help you to develop an interest in mathematics and within no time, you will become an expert...

1 The *Sutras*

Sutras or Aphorisms are nothing but Word formulae. They describe the simple ways to solve arithmetical problems. These *sutras* are also divided into *sub-sutras* or corollaries. Vedic Mathematics consists of 16 *sutras* as described below.

1. ***Ekadhikena Purvena:*** The first *sutra* of Vedic Mathematics, ***Ekadhikena Purvena***, means *"By one more than the previous one"*. Its corollary is ***Anurupyena*** *(proportionality)*.

2. ***Nikhilam Navatashcaramam Dashatah:*** This *sutra* means *"All from 9 and the last from 10"*. Its corollary is ***Sisyate Sesasamjnah*** (Remainder remains constant).

3. ***Urdhva-Tiryagbyham***: This *sutra* means *"Vertically and crosswise"*. Its corollary is ***Adyamadyenantyamantyena*** *(The First by the First and the Last by the Last)*.

4. ***Paraavartya Yojayet:*** This *sutra* means *"Transpose and adjust"*. *Its corollary is* ***Kevalaih Saptakam Gunyat*** *(For 7, the Multiplicand is 143)*.

5. ***Shunyam Saamyasamuccaye:*** This sutra means *"When the samuccaya is the same that samuccaya is zero"*. *Its corollary is* ***Vestanam*** *(Osculation)*.

6. ***Anurupye – Shunyamanyat:*** This *sutra* means *"If one is in ratio, the other is zero"*. *Its corollary is* ***Yavadunam Tavadunam*** (Whatever the extent of

its deficiency, lessen it still further to that very extent).

7. ***Sankalana - Vyavakalanabhyam:*** This *sutra* means *"By addition and by subtraction"*. Its *corollary is* **Yavadunam Tavadunikritya Varga Yojayet** (*Whatever the Deficit, Subtract that Deficit from the Number and Write alongside the Square of that Deficit).*

8. ***Puranapuranabyham:*** This *sutra* means *"By the completion or non-completion"*. Its *corollary is* **Antyayor Dashakepi** (*Whose last digits together total 10 and whose previous part is exactly the same).*

9. ***Chalana-Kalanabyham:*** *This sutra means "Differences and Similarities"*. Its *corollary is* **Antyayoreva** *(Only the last term).*

10. **Yaavadunam:** This *sutra* means *"Whatever the extent of its deficiency"*. Its *corollary is* **Samuccayagunitah** (The sum of the coefficients in the product).

11. **Vyashtisamanstih:** This *sutra* means *"Part and Whole"*. Its corollary is **Lopanasthapanabhyam** (*By Alternate Elimination and Retention).*

12. ***Sheshanyankena Charamena:*** This *sutra* means *"The remainders by the last digit"*. Its *corollary is* **Vilokanam** (*By mere observation).*

13. ***Sopaantyadvayamantyam:*** *This sutra means "The ultimate and twice the penultimate".*

Its corollary is **Gunitasamuccayah Samuccayagunitah** *(The product of the sum of the coefficients in the factors is equal to the sum of the coefficients in the product).*

14. ***Ekanyunena Purvena:*** This *sutra* means *"By one less than the previous one"*. *Its corollary is* **Dhvajanka** (on top of the flag).

15. ***Gunitasamuchyah:*** *This sutra means "The product of the sum is equal to the sum of the product". Its corollary is* **Dwandwa Yoga**.

16. ***Gunakasamuchyah:*** *This sutra means "The factors of the sum is equal to the sum of the factors". Its corollary is* **Adyam Antyam Madhyam**.

With the help of some of the above *sutras*, you can achieve astonishing results in day to day arithmetic, as well as in numerous entrance exams. In the following chapters, I have taken utmost care to present these *sutras* in their most practical form, and to only consider those *sutra s* which will really be helpful in practical applications.

2 Single Digit Multiplication

Let's begin our learning with the most basic arithmetical problem. These days, students tend to learn multiplication tables till 20 or 30. But learning these multiplication tables is a tedious task, and it's not even required. I will prove this in the present as well as the forthcoming chapters through some interesting techniques. To help us with single digit multiplication, we have the *Nikhilam Sutra* on hand.

Nikhilam Sutra

As explained in the previous chapter, this *sutra* means *"All from 9 and the last from 10"*. This is one of the most useful *sutras* in Vedic Mathematics. We can directly apply it to multiply single digit numbers as shown below.

Example: Multiply 8 by 7

Step 1 :   Take the nearest power of 10 for these numbers. Powers of 10 are 10, 100, 1000, 10000...
Thus, the nearest power of 10 for the numbers 8 and 7 is 10.

Step 2 :   Write down the numbers as shown below:

    8

    <u>7</u>

Step 3 :   Subtract both the numbers from the base 10 and write the result on the right side with a minus sign (-) in front of them to indicate that they are less than 10 or negative as shown below.

$$\begin{array}{cc} \mathbf{8} & -2 \\ \mathbf{7} & -3 \end{array}$$

Step 4 : Multiply the 2 deficit figures on the right (-2 and -3). Product 6 is the right-hand side part of the answer.

The right-side of the answer is 1 digit only, since here, we are taking the base as 10 (the *first* power of 10). Similarly, if you are taking the base as 100, then the right side of the answer should be 2 digits.

$$\begin{array}{c|c} \mathbf{8} & \textit{-2} \\ \mathbf{7} & \textit{-3} \\ \hline & \textit{6} \end{array}$$

Step 5 : The left hand side number of the answer is obtained by any of following methods:

(a) Do cross-wise addition

$8 + (-3) = \mathbf{5}$

$$\begin{array}{c|c} \mathbf{8} & \textit{-2} \\ \mathbf{7} & \textit{-3} \\ \hline \mathbf{5} & \mathbf{6} \end{array}$$

(b) Do cross-wise addition

$7 + (-2) = \mathbf{5}$

$$\begin{array}{c|c} \mathbf{8} & \textit{-2} \\ \mathbf{7} & \textit{-3} \\ \hline \mathbf{5} & \mathbf{6} \end{array}$$

Now write this as the left side number of the answer. Thus, the answer is **56**.

Let us now solve some more problems of a similar type.

Example: Find the product of: 6 x 9

We can again take the base as 10. Actually, all single digit numbers have base as 10, because they are nearer to 10 than 100.

$$
\begin{array}{ll}
6 & \textit{-4} \\
9 & \textit{-1} \\
\hline
\end{array}
$$

Step 1   :   We take 10 as base. Subtract 6 and 9 from 10 and write the answer on the right side, as shown above.

Step 2   :   Multiply the digits on the right side (-4 x -1 = **4**). Write this answer on the right-hand side.

$$
\begin{array}{ll}
6 & \textit{-4} \\
9 & \textit{-1} \\
\hline
 & \mid \quad 4 \\
\end{array}
$$

Step 3   :   Do either **6 – 1** or **9 – 4**, you will get same answer, **5**. Write this digit on the left-side of the answer.

$$
\begin{array}{ll}
6 & \textit{-4} \\
9 & \textit{-1} \\
\hline
5 & \mid \quad 4 \\
\end{array}
$$

Thus, the answer is **54**.

Example: Find the product of: 4 x 6
Take the base as 10.

$$
\begin{array}{ll}
4 & \textit{-6} \\
6 & \textit{-4} \\
\hline
\end{array}
$$

Step 1 : We take 10 as the base. Subtract 4 and 6 from 10 and write the answer on the right side, as shown above.

Step 2 : Multiply the digits on the right side (-6 x -4 = 24). This is a 2 digit answer. But we can write only 1 digit on the right side. So from **24**, write the last digit in the units place i.e. **4** on the right hand side. The digit **2**, we can use as the carry over, and we will add this **2** to the left-side digit that we get.

```
4       -6

6       -4
_____
         4
```

Step 3 : Do either **4 – 4** or **6 – 6**, you will get same answer, **0**. Add the carry over, 2, from Step-2. And 0 + 2 = **2**. Write this digit on the left-side of the answer.

```
2  |  4
```

Thus, the answer is **24**.

Example: Find the product of: 6 x 6

Take the base as 10.

Following the above steps:

```
6        -4
   ╳
6        -4
_____
3   |   6
```

Thus, the answer is **36**.

Example: Find the product of: 8 x 8

Take the base as 10.

Following the above steps:

$$
\begin{array}{c|c}
8 \quad \searrow -2 & \\
8 \quad \nearrow -2 & \\
\hline
6 & 4 \\
\end{array}
$$

Thus, the answer is **64**.

Exercise 1:

_____

(A) Find the product of the following numbers:

1) 8 x 9

2) 9 x 3

3) 4 x 3

(B) Fill in the blanks:

1) 5 x 5 = _____

2) 8 x 5 = _____

3) 7 x 3 = _____

****

3 Multiplication of 2 or more digit numbers with *Nikhilam* Technique

We have already used the ***Nikhilam*** Technique to multiply single-digit numbers. The same technique can be used to multiply 2 or more digit numbers, with speed and accuracy. But, I suggest using this method only if the numbers are near the power of 10. This means that you can use this method very effectively if both the numbers are near 10, 100, 1000, 10000 and so on. This technique can be used for other type of numbers also, but it will take more time. We have a different technique for such numbers. For the time being, let's use the ***Nikhilam Sutra*** for the numbers near the power of 10.

Example: Find the product of 96 x 95.

Here, base is 100, as both the numbers are near 100. Now following the rules, the method is as follows:

$$
\begin{array}{r}
96 \quad\quad -04 \\
x \quad 95 \quad\quad -05 \\
\hline
(96\text{-}05) \text{ or} \ \Big| \ 4 \times 5 \\
(95\text{-}04) \\
\hline
\text{Answer} = 91 \ \Big| \ 20 \\
= \mathbf{9120}
\end{array}
$$

Step 1 : Both the numbers, 96 and 95 are near 100, second power of 10, which becomes our base.

Step 2 : Write the deviation on the right of the numbers, i.e., (96 – 100 = -4) and (95 – 100 = -5)

Step 3 : Multiply both the deviations.
-4 x -5 = **20**. This is the right side of answer.

Here, you will notice, the right-side of the answer is 2 digits. This is because we are taking the base (in Step 1), as 100. Since 100 is *second* power of 10, the right side of the answer should be of 2 digits.

Step 4 : On the left side, go cross-wise i.e. 96 – 5 or 95 – 4. Both equal **91**. Combining these two, we get the answer = **9120**.

Example: Find the product of 14 x 11.

Here, we will use the base as 10, as both the numbers are near 10.

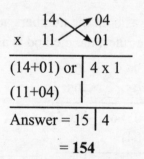

$$
\begin{array}{c|c}
14 \diagdown \nearrow 04 & \\
x \quad 11 \diagup \nwarrow 01 & \\
\hline
(14+01) \text{ or} & 4 \times 1 \\
(11+04) & \\
\hline
\text{Answer} = 15 & 4
\end{array}
$$

= **154**

Step 1 : Both the numbers, 14 and 11 are near 10, first power of 10, which becomes our base.

Step 2 : Write the deviation on the right of the numbers, i.e., (14 – 10 = 4) and (11 – 10 = 1). Note that the deviation 4 and 1, both are positive. Whereas, in all the earlier examples, the deviation was negative.

Step 3 : Multiply both the deviations. 4 x 1 = **4**. This is the right side of answer.

Step 4 : Now we have to add (not Subtract) cross-wise, since the deviation is positive. On the left side, go cross-wise i.e. 14 +1 or 11 + 4. Both equal **15**. We get two parts as 15 & 4.

Thus, we get the answer = **154**.

Example: Find the product of 13 x 7.

Here, we will use the base as 10, as both the numbers are near 10.

$$
\begin{array}{r}
13 \qquad 03 \\
\text{x } 7 \quad - 03 \\
\hline
(13\text{-}3) \text{ or } \big| \; 3 \text{ x } \text{-}3 \\
(7\text{+}3) \\
\hline
= 10 \; \big| \; \overline{9} \\
= 100\text{-}9 = \mathbf{91}
\end{array}
$$

Step 1 : Both the numbers, 13 and 7 are near 10, first power of 10, which becomes our base. But there is one thing different in this problem, one number is greater than 10 and the other number is less than 10.

Step 2 : In this case, one deviation will be positive and other deviation will be negative. Write the deviation on the right of the numbers i.e. (13 - 10 = 3) and (7 – 10 = -3)

Step 3 : Multiply both the deviations. 3 x -3 = **-9**. This is right side of answer.

17

Step 4 : On left side, go cross-wise i.e., 13 - 3 or 7 + 3. Both equal 10. We get two parts as 10 & -9. There is a clear problem out here.

How can -9 be a part of the answer?

Well, this brings us to a very interesting technique of Vedic Mathematics - *Vinculum Numbers*. The secret to *Vinculum Numbers* lies in the *sutras,* *"Nikhilam Navatashcaramam Dashatah"* *(All from 9 the Last from 10)* and the *"Ekadhikena Purvena"* *(By one more than the previous one)*. These *sutras* are used to obtain *Vinculum Numbers*.

Vinculum Numbers are explained in detail, in a separate chapter. But for solving this problem, here is a small explanation.

Vinculum: *The numbers, which by presentation, contain both positive and negative digits, are called Vinculum numbers.*

Thus, a number 7 can be represented as 10-3 or **13** and vice-versa.

So the solution to our problem is to convert the *Vinculum number* to a normal one.

10 | 9 = **(100-9) = 91**

If *Vinculum numbers* have made you a little confused, please feel free to have a look at the chapter dealing with them.

Numbers away from power of 10:

Now, let us look at the multiplication of the numbers which are not near the power of 10. We just have to follow one rule in this case. Rest of the method remains the same.

Rule: *If R.H.S. (right-hand side number) contains less number of digits than the number of zeros in the base, then the remaining digits are filled up by giving zero or zeroes on the left side of the R.H.S. If the number of digits are more than the number of zeroes in the base, the excess digit or digits are to be added to L.H.S of the answer.*

The general form of multiplication under *Nikhilam* can be shown as follows:

Let N_1 and N_2 be two numbers near a given base in powers of 10, and D_1 and D_2 are their respective deviations from the base. Then, $N_1 \times N_2$ can be represented as

N1	D1	
N2	D2	
(N1 + D2) or		D1 x D2
(N2 + D1)		

If the rule seems complex at present, things will become clear once you will see the examples.

Example: Find the product of 75 x 95.

Here, we will use the base as 100, as both the numbers are near 100.

$$
\begin{array}{r|l}
75 & -25 \\
\times \; 95 & -05 \\
\hline
(75\text{-}05) \text{ or} & -25 \times -5 \\
(95\text{-}25) & \\
\hline
= 70 & 125 \\
= (70\text{+}1) & 25 \text{ (observe the rule)} \\
= \mathbf{7125} &
\end{array}
$$

Step 1 : Both the numbers, 75 and 95 are near 100, second power of 10, which becomes our base.

Step 2 : Write the deviation on the right side of the numbers, i.e., (75 − 100 = -25) and (95 − 100 = -5)

Step 3 : Multiply both the deviations. -25 x -5 = 125. This is the right side of the answer.

Step 4 : On left side, go cross-wise i.e. 75 − 5 or 95 − 25. Both equal 70. We get two parts as 70 & 125. Now, according to the rule given above, we remove the first digit from 125, which is 1 and add it to the left-hand side number, 70 + 1 = 71. Thus, we have now 2 new parts of the answer, **71** and **25**.

Thus, we get the answer = **7125**.

Example: Find the product of 750 x 995.

Here, we will use the base as 1000, as both the numbers are near 1000.

$$
\begin{array}{rl}
750 & -250 \\
\text{x } 995 & -005
\end{array}
$$

$$
\frac{(750\text{-}005) \text{ or} \mid -250 \text{ x -5}}{(995\text{-}250)}
$$

$$
\frac{= 745 \mid 1250 \text{ (observe the rule)}}{= \mathbf{746250}}
$$

Step 1 : Both the numbers 750 and 995 are near 1000, third power of 10, which becomes our base.

Step 2 : Write the deviation on right of the numbers, i.e. (750 – 1000 = -250) and (995 – 1000 = -5)

Step 3 : Multiply both the deviations. -250 x -5 = 1250. This is the right side of the answer.

Step 4 : On the left side, go cross-wise i.e. 750 – 5 or 995 – 250. Both equal 745. We get two parts as 745 & 1250. Observe rule as well as step-4 of previous problem. So, we get 2 new parts of answer: **746** and **250**.

Thus, we get the answer = **746250**.

Example: Find the product of 1275 x 1004.

Here, we will use the base as 1000, as both the numbers are near 1000.

$$
\begin{array}{c|c}
1275 & 275 \\
1004 & 004 \\
\hline
1279 & 275 \times 4 \\
\hline
\end{array}
$$

= 1279 | 1100 (observe the rule)
= **1280100**

Step 1 : Both the numbers 1275 and 1004 are near 1000, third power of 10, which becomes our base.

21

Step 2 : Write the deviation on the right side of the numbers, i.e. (1275 – 1000 = 275) and (1004 – 1000 = 4)

Step 3 : Multiply both the deviations. 275 x 4 = 1100. This is the right side of answer.

Step 4 : On the left side, go cross-wise i.e. 1275 + 4 or 1004 + 275. Both equal 1279. We get two parts as 1279 & 1100. According to the rule, we get 2 new parts of answer: **1280** and **110**. Thus, we get the answer = **1280100**.

Exercise 2:

(A) Find the product of the following numbers:

   1) 97 x 87

   2) 1235 x 1001

   3) 1005 x 99 5

(B) Fill in the blanks:

   1) 99 x 89   = _____

   2) 1105 x 1005 = _____

   3) 1100 x 990   = _____

****

4 Multiplication by Series of 9

We now look into the more specific numbers. Here, we will learn a new technique how to multiply any number with a number from the series of 9. The aphorism *"One less than the previous one"*, which is described by the *sutra* *"Ekanyunena Purvena"*, is used in the process of multiplication of any number with the number in the series of 9. The numbers in the series of 9 are: 9, 99, 999, 9999, and so on. Let us now have a look at the example.

Example: Find the product of 7 x 9

Method :

Step 1 : The left-hand side digit (digits) of the answer is obtained by subtracting 1 from the number. Here, the number to be multiplied with 9 is **7**. So, the left side digit is obtained as shown:

7 – 1 = **6** (L.H.S. digit)

Step 2 : The right-hand side digit is obtained by subtracting the digit obtained in step-1 (number 6) from another number (number 9), as shown below:

9 – 6 = 3.

Step 3 : The two numbers obtained are 6 and 3. Thus, the answer is: **63.**

Example: Find the product of: 6 x 9

Step 1 : 6 – 1 = **5** (L.H.S. Digit)

Step 2 : 9 – 5 = **4** (R.H.S. Digit)

Step 3 : The answer is **54**

Example: Find the product of: 12 x 99

Step 1 : 12 – 1 = **11**

Step 2 : 99 – 11 = **88**

Step 3 : The answer is **1188**

Example: Find the product of: 24 x 99

Step 1 : 24 – 1 = **23**

Step 2 : 99 – 23 = **76**

Step 3 : The answer is **2376**

Example: Find the product of: 356 x 999

Step 1 : 356 – 1 = **355**

Step 2 : 999 – 355 = **644**

Step 3 : The answer is **355644**

Example: Find the product of: 878 x 9999

Step 1 : 878 – 1 = **877**

Step 2 : 9999 – 877 = **9122**

Step 3 : The answer is **8779122**

Exercise 3:

(A) Find the products using "Ekanyunena Purvena" (Multiply by series of 9) process:

1) 58 x 99

2) 427 x 999

3) 2482 x 9999

(B) Fill in the blanks:

1) 9 x 99   = _____

2) 100 x 999   = _____

3) 1999 x 9999 = _____

****

5   Multiplication by 11

Let us, once again, learn a new technique related to specific numbers. Suppose, you are caught in a specific scenario of multiplying a 2 - digit number with 11, then you can use a short-cut method to get the product in mere seconds. There is a common and effective method of multiplying a 2-digit number with 11, by using one of the corollaries of the *sutra* ***"Urdhva-Tiryagbhyam"***

Consider the following example:

Example: Find the product of 45 x 11

You can use following steps to obtain the answer:

Step 1   :   Divide the Product in 3 parts. (In your mind or on a paper)

$$\begin{array}{ccc} & 4 & 5 \\ x & 1 & 1 \\ \hline & | & | \\ \hline \end{array}$$

Step 2   :   In the last part, write the last digit of the number that you want to multiply with 11. In this case, last digit of 45, i.e. 5.

$$\begin{array}{ccc} & 4 & 5 \\ x & 1 & 1 \\ \hline & & 5 \\ \hline \end{array}$$

Step 3 : In the middle part, write the sum of both the digits of a number that you want to multiply with 11. In this case, the sum of digits of number 45, i.e. **4 + 5 = 9**

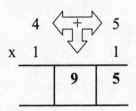

Step 4 : In the first part, write the first digit of the number that you want to multiply with 11 (added with carry, if any). Here, first digit of 45, i.e. 4. and middle digit is 9, a single digit number. So, no carry is generated. So, write 4 in the first part.

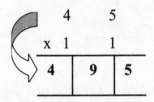

Thus, the product of **45 x 11 = 495.**

Consider another example:

Example: 98 x 11

Again follow the above mentioned steps to obtain the answer:

Step 1 : Divide the Product in 3 parts.

Step 2 : In the last part, write the last digit of the number that you want to multiply with 11. In this case, last digit of 98, i.e. 8.

9	8
x 1	1
	8

Step 3 : In the middle part, write the sum of both the digits of a number that you want to multiply with 11. In this case, the sum of the digits of number 98, i.e., **9 + 8 = 17.** This is a two digit number. So, write second digit, i.e. 7 in the middle part and take first digit, i.e. 1 as a carry.

9	8
x 1	1
7	**8**

CARRY ⟶ **1**

Step 4 : In the first part, write the first digit of the number that you want to multiply with 11 (added with carry, if any). Here, the first digit of 98, i.e. 9 and carry is 1. So, add the carry generated to the first number, i.e.**9 + 1 = 10.**So, write **10** in the first part.

9	8
x 1	1
	8

Thus, the product of **98 x 11 = 1078.**

28

Exercise 4:

(A) Find the products in the following cases with the use of '*Multiply by 11*' method:

        1) 25 x 11

        2) 77 x 11

        3) 99 x 11

(B) Fill in the blanks:

        1) 90 x 11 = _____

        2) 87 x 11 = _____

        3) 49 x 11 = _____

****

6 General Method for Multiplication

We have already seen many techniques to multiply specific numbers. Now, let us look at one technique of multiplication which you can use to multiply any general numbers. This technique is described by the *sutra "Urdhva - Tiryagbhyam"*.

The *sutra "Urdhva – Tiryagbhyam"* is described by the aphorism *"Vertically and Cross-wise."* *Urdhva–Tiryagbhyam* is the general formula applicable to all cases of multiplication and also in the division of a large number by another large number. Let us now look at few examples.

(i) Multiplication of two 2 digit numbers:

Example: Find the product of 15 x 11

Symbolically we can represent the process as follows:

The symbols are operated from right to left.

Step 1 : The right hand most digit of the multiplicand, the first number (15) i.e. 5 is multiplied by the right hand most digit of the multiplier, the second number (11) i.e. 1. The product 5 x 1 = 5 forms the right hand most part of the answer.

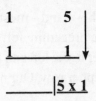

$$\begin{array}{c|c} 1 & 5 \\ 1 & 1 \\ \hline & 5 \times 1 \end{array}$$

Step 2 : Now, diagonally multiply the first digit of the multiplicand (15) i.e. 5 and second digit of the multiplier (11) i.e. 1 (answer 5 x 1 = 5); then multiply the second digit of the multiplicand i.e. 1 and first digit of the multiplier i.e. 1 (answer 1 x 1 = 1) ; add these two i.e. 5 + 1 = 6. It gives the next, i.e., second digit of the answer. Here the second digit of the answer is 6.

$$\underline{1 + 5}\big|5$$

Step 3 : Now, multiply the second digit of the multiplicand i.e. 1 and second digit of the multiplier i.e. 1 vertically, i.e. 1 x 1 = 1. It gives the left hand most part of the answer.

$$\begin{array}{c|c} 1 & 5 \\ \downarrow & \\ 1 & 1 \end{array}$$

$$\underline{1 \times 1}\big|\,6\,\big|\,5 = 165$$

Thus, the answer is **165.**

What happens when one of the results i.e. either in the last digit or in the middle digit of the result, contains more than 1 digit?

31

Answer is simple. The right – hand – most digit should be put down there and the preceding left –hand –side digit should be carried over to the left and placed under the previous digit of the upper row. Our next example will make it clear.

Example: Find the product of 28 x 35.

Step 1   :   8 x 5 = 40. 0 is retained as the first digit of the answer and 4 is carried over.

$$
\begin{array}{ll}
\mathbf{2} & \mathbf{8} \\
\underline{\mathbf{3}} & \underline{\mathbf{5}} \\
\end{array}
$$

Carry ->   4
_____|_**0**

Step 2   :   2 x 5 = 10; 8 x 3 = 24; 10 + 24 = 34; add the carry over 4 to 34. Now, the result is 34 + 4 = 38. Here, 8 is retained as the second digit of the answer and 3 is carried over.

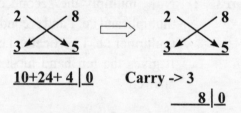

$$\underline{10+24+\ 4}\ |\ \underline{0} \qquad \textbf{Carry -> 3}$$

$$\underline{\hspace{2cm} 8}\ |\ \underline{0}$$

Step 3   :   2 x 3 = 6; add the carry over 3 to 6. The result 6 + 3 = 9 is the third or final digit from right to left of the answer.

$$
\begin{array}{ll}
\Big\downarrow\ \mathbf{2} & \mathbf{8} \\
\Big\downarrow\ \underline{\mathbf{3}} & \underline{\mathbf{5}} \\
\end{array}
\quad\Longrightarrow\quad
\begin{array}{ll}
\Big\downarrow\ \mathbf{2} & \mathbf{8} \\
\Big\downarrow\ \underline{\mathbf{3}} & \underline{\mathbf{5}} \\
\end{array}
$$

$$\underline{6+3+\ }\ |\ \underline{\mathbf{8}}\ |\ \underline{0} \qquad \underline{\mathbf{9}}\ |\ \underline{\mathbf{8}}\ |\ \underline{0}$$

   Thus 28 x 35 = **980**

Example: Find the product of 48 x 47

```
        4       8
    x   4       7
   ─────────────────
        1   6   0   6
Carry →     6   5
   ─────────────────
        2   2   5   6
```

Step 1 : 8 x 7 = 56;

6 is written in the answer and 5 the carried over digit, is placed below the second digit.

Step 2 : (4 x 7) + (8 x 4) = 28 + 32 = 60;

60 is the answer. It is added with the carry over digit 5. So, the answer is 65. 5 is written in the answer and 6, the carry over digit is placed below the third digit.

Step 3 : 4 x 4 = 16. The carry over digit 6 is added to this. Thus, 16 + 6 = 22 is written in the answer.

Thus, the answer is **2256**.

(ii) Multiplication of two 3 digit numbers:

Example: Find the product of 124 x 132.

Proceeding from right to left

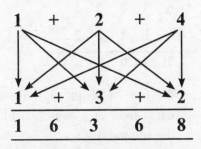

33

Step 1 : $4 \times 2 = 8$. First digit = **8**

Step 2 : $(2 \times 2) + (3 \times 4) = 4 + 12 = 16$.
The digit 6 is retained and 1 is carried over to left side. Second digit = **6**.

Step 3 : $(1 \times 2) + (2 \times 3) + (1 \times 4) =$
$2 + 6 + 4 = 12$.
The carry over 1 of the step above is added i.e. $12 + 1 = 13$. Now 3 is retained and 1 is carried over to the left side.
Thus, the third digit = **3**.

Step 4 : $(1 \times 3) + (2 \times 1) = 3 + 2 = 5$.
The carry over 1 of the step above is added i.e. $5 + 1 = 6$. It is retained.
Thus, the fourth digit = **6**

Step 5 : $(1 \times 1) = 1$. As there is no carry over number from the previous step, it is retained. Thus, the fifth digit = **1**

Thus, **124 x 132 = 16368.**

Let us work on another problem by placing the carried over digits under the first row and proceed.

Example: Find the product of 234 x 316

	2		3		4
x	3		1		6
	6	1	7	2	4
Carry ->		1	2	2	2
	7	3	9	4	4

Step 1 : $4 \times 6 = 24$. Right digit answer is 4 and carry over is 2, which is placed below the second digit.

34

Step 2 : $(3 \times 6) + (4 \times 1) = 18 + 4 = 22$; 2, the carry over digit is placed below the third digit.

Step 3 : $(2 \times 6) + (3 \times 1) + (4 \times 3) =$

$12 + 3 + 12 = 27$; 2, the carry over digit is placed below the fourth digit.

Step 4 : $(2 \times 1) + (3 \times 3) = 2+9 = 11$; 1, carry over digit is placed below fifth digit.

Step 5 : $(2 \times 3) = 6$.

Step 6 : Respective digits are added to get the answer.

Exercise 5:

(A) Find the products using *Urdhva Tiryagbhyam* (Vertically and Cross-wise) process:

    1) **25 x 16**

    2) **137 x 214**

    3) **452 x 398**

(B) Fill in the blanks:

    1) **29 x 13** = _____

    2) **97 x 98** = _____

    3) **139 x 351** = _____

****

7   Vinculum Numbers

The numbers, which by presentation, contain both positive and negative digits, are called *Vinculum Numbers*.

In Vedic Mathematics, there exists a way to write higher numbers (6, 7, 8, 9) in terms of lower numbers (0, 1, 2, 3, 4). It's important, because it makes difficult problems fairly simple, and it is much easier to work with the lower numbers, especially in multiplication. For using this method, we only need to know multiplication tables up to 5 x 5. This method of writing numbers is called *Vinculum Numbers*, and results in numbers containing both, positive and negative digits.

How to get *Vinculum Numbers*?

The secret to *Vinculum Numbers* lies in the *"Nikhilam Navatashcaramam Dashatah"* sutra (All from 9 the Last from 10) and the *"Ekadhikena Purvena"* sutra (By one more than the previous one). These *sutras* are used to obtain the *Vinculum Numbers*.

Conversion of general numbers into *Vinculum Numbers*:

We obtain them by converting the digits which are 5, above 5 or less than 5 without changing the value of that number.

Consider a number '8'. (Note, it is greater than 5).

Step 1   :   Decide the base. In case of 8, the base will be 10, since it's the nearest.

Step 2 : Use the complement (*purak - rekhank*) from 10 (the base). The complement of 8 from the base 10 will be **2** (since 10 - 8 = 2).

Step 3 : Write 2 (with bar on top), to represent units place.

Step 4 : Now, since the base is a 2 digit number, add 1 to the left (i.e. tens place).

This gives us: $8 = 08 = 1\overline{2}$.

Accordingly, we can think and write it in the following way

General Number	Conversion	Vinculum Number
6	10 - 4	$1\overline{4}$
97	100 - 3	$10\overline{3}$
289	300 - 11	$31\overline{1}$

Example: 98 x 92

$$98 = 100 - 2 = 10\overline{2}$$

$$92 = 100 - 8 = 10\overline{8}$$

Now

$$
\begin{array}{r}
1\ 0\ \overline{2} \\
\times\ \ 1\ 0\ \overline{8} \\
\hline
1\ 0\ \overline{0}\ 0\ 6 \\
\overline{1}\ \ 1 \qquad \leftarrow Carry \\
\hline
1\ \overline{1}\ 0\ 1\ 6 = \mathbf{9016}
\end{array}
$$

37

Steps to solve the above problem:

Step 1 : Obtain the *Vinculum Number* from the given two numbers.

i.e., Vinculum of 98 = $10\overline{2}$

Vinculum of 92 = $10\overline{8}$

Step 2 : Proceed by the *"Vertically and Cross-wise"* method, described in the previous chapter. See Multiplication of 3 digit numbers.

Hence, this method uses the above mentioned techniques and rules to find the product, except that it first finds the Vinculum number from the given number and then proceeds normally.

Example 24: 99 x 99

Step 1: Find the Vinculum of the numbers given.

i.e., Vinculum of 99 = $10\overline{1}$

Step 2 : Proceed by the *"Vertically and Cross-wise"* method, described in the previous chapter. See Multiplication of 3 digit numbers.

Hence, this method uses the above mentioned techniques and rules to find the product, except that it first finds the Vinculum number from the given number and then proceeds normally.

Example 24 :   99 x 99

Step 1   :   Find the Vinculum of the numbers given.

i.e., Vinculum of 99 = 10$\overline{1}$

Step 2   :   Proceed by the *"Vertically and Cross-wise"* method, described in previous chapter. See Multiplication of 3 digit numbers.

99 = 100 - 1 = 101

Now 99 x 99 is

$$1\ 0\ \overline{1}$$
$$x\quad 1\ 0\ \overline{1}$$
$$\overline{}$$
$$1\ \overline{0}\ 2\ 0\ 1 = \mathbf{9801}$$

****

8 Division by *Nikhilam*

After having used various multiplication techniques, let us now look at the techniques that Vedic Mathematics has provided us, to perform Division. The aphorism "*All from nine, Last from ten*", described by the *sutra* "***Nikhilam Navatashcaramam Dashatah***" has been effectively used by us for multiplication. Now, same rules can be applied for the division process, which we will see in this chapter.

Nikhilam for Division:

(i) Two digit numbers:

Consider some two digit numbers (dividend) and divisor 9. Observe the following example very carefully.

i) $12 \div 9$

The Quotient **(Q) is 1**; Remainder **(R) is 3**.

Since   **9) 12 (1**

$$\frac{9}{3}$$

ii) $41 \div 9$, Q is **4**, R is **5**.

iii) $71 \div 9$, Q is **7**, R is **8**.

Now, we have another type of representation for the above examples as given hereunder:

Step 1   :   Split each dividend into a left hand part for the Quotient and a right - hand part for the remainder by a slant line or slash.

E.g.:   12 as 1 | 2

40

Step 2 : Leave some space below such representation, draw a horizontal line.

E.g.: $\underline{1\mid 2}$

Step 3 : Put the first digit of the dividend as it is under the horizontal line. Put the same digit under the right hand part for the remainder; add the two and place the sum i.e., sum of the digits of the numbers as the remainder.

E.g.
$$\begin{array}{c|c} 1 & 2 \\ & 1 \\ \hline 1 & 3 \end{array}$$

Now, the problem is over. i.e,

$$12 \div 9 \text{ gives } Q = 1, R = 3$$
$$41 \div 9 \text{ gives } Q = 4, R = 5$$
$$71 \div 9 \text{ gives } Q = 7, R = 8$$

Proceeding for some more of the two digit number division by 9, we get

a) $21 \div 9$ as

$$9)\ \begin{array}{c|c} 2 & 1 \\ 2 & \\ \hline 2 & 3 \end{array} \quad \text{i.e.} \quad Q=2, R=3$$

b) $43 \div 9$ as

$$9)\ \begin{array}{c|c} 4 & 3 \\ 4 & \\ \hline 4 & 7 \end{array} \quad \text{i.e.} \quad Q = 4, R = 7.$$

The examples given so far convey that in the division of two digit numbers by 9, we can mechanically take the first digit down for the quotient – column and that, by adding the quotient to the second digit, we can get the remainder. But, take a look at the problem mentioned below:

Consider the following problem:

$$48 \div 9$$

Here, you will write: Q = 4

R = (4+8) = 12

But how can a remainder be greater than a divisor? So, this answer is wrong!!!

Don't worry. If you get a remainder(R) greater than divisor (9), then simply subtract 9 from the remainder and rewrite the remainder. Then, add 1 to the Quotient (Q).

In above case, this is what you can do:

R = 12-9

R = 3   and

Q = 4+1

Q = 5

So, new values for

$$48 \div 9 \quad Q = 5$$

R = 3

(ii) More than 2 digit numbers:

Let us see some examples for division of 3 digit numbers. Note that the remainder is the sum of the digits of the dividend. The first digit of the dividend from the left is added mechanically to the second digit of the dividend to obtain the second digit of the quotient. This digit, added to the third digit sets the remainder. The first digit of the dividend remains as the first digit of the quotient.

Consider   **520 ÷ 9**

Add the first digit, 5 to second digit, 2 getting 5 + 2 = 7. Hence Quotient is 57. Now, second digit of 57 i.e. 7 is added to third digit 0 of dividend to get the remainder i.e. 7 + 0 = 7

Thus
$$9) \quad \begin{array}{c|c} 52 & 0 \\ 5 & 7 \\ \hline 57 & 7 \end{array}$$

Q is 57, R is 7.

Extending the same principle even to bigger numbers of more digits, we can get the results.

Example :   **1204 ÷ 9**

Step 1 :   Partition the dividend into two parts. The digits in the right part must be equal to digits in divisor. So, 1204 becomes 120 | 4

Step 2 :   Set up a temporary quotient of first digit. So, now quotient is 1. Add first digit 1 to the second digit, 2, 1+2 = 3. So, now quotient is 13.

Step 3 :   Add the second digit of temporary quotient 13. i.e. 3 to third digit of dividend, '0' and obtain the Quotient. 3 + 0 = 3. So, Q = 133. As first partition of dividend is over, you have got the quotient.

43

Step 4 : Add the third digit of Quotient 133 i.e. 3 to digit in second partition, '4' of the dividend. So, Remainder, R = 3 + 4= 7, and Q = 133.

In symbolic form

$$9) \overline{ \begin{array}{c|c} 120 & 4 \\ 13 & 3 \\ \hline 133 & 7 \end{array} }$$

Exercise 6:

(A) Obtain the Quotient and Remainder for the following problems:

1) $52 \div 9$

2) $340 \div 9$

3) $6210 \div 9$

(B) Fill in the blanks:

1) $39 \div 9$ = _____

2) $241 \div 9$ = _____

3) $5712 \div 9$ = _____

****

44

9 Division by *'Remainders by The Last Digit'*

Let us now look at a very specific and precision related technique of Division. When a very high precision is expected in the calculation, *"Remainders by the Last Digit"* helps us to solve the problem.

The aphorism *"The remainders by the Last Digit"* is described by the *sutra* *"Shesanyankena Charamena."* *Shesanyankena Charamena* is the twelfth *sutra* of Vedic Mathematics. This *sutra* can be used to express a fraction as a decimal, to all its decimal places.

Example: Express 1/7 as a decimal

Step 1 : Add a zero to numerator: 1 (i.e. now numerator is 10, and NOT 1)

Step 2 : If this number is less than the denominator, add another zero. If it is greater than the denominator, proceed to the next step.

Step 3 : Divide this number by the denominator and pay attention to the quotient. 10 / 7 = **1** is the quotient with a remainder of **3**

Step 4 : Add a zero to this remainder and divide it by the denominator: 30 / 7 = **4** is the quotient with a remainder of **2**

Step 5 : Add a zero to this remainder and divide it by the denominator: 20 / 7 = **2** is the quotient with a remainder of **6**

Step 6 : Add a zero to this remainder and divide it by the denominator: 60 / 7 = **8** is the quotient with a remainder of **4**

Step 7 : Add a zero to this remainder and divide it by the denominator: 40 / 7 = **5** is the quotient with a remainder of **5**

Step 8 : Add a zero to this remainder and divide it by the denominator: 50 / 7 = **7** is the quotient with a remainder of **1**

Step 9 : At this point, notice that this remainder (**1**) is the same number as the numerator. The answer is going to repeat from here on end, so we'll stop.

Step 10 : Write these quotients in order, obtained from step-3 onwards. They are as follows: **1, 4, 2, 8, 5, 7, 1...**

Step 11 : Now club these digits and place '**0.**' in front of them, 0.142857142857...

Step 12 : Thus, 1/7 = 0.142857142857 repeating.

Exercise 7:

Find the decimal form for the problem using *Remainders by The Last Digit* method:

1) 1 / 8

2) 1 / 5

3) 1 / 9

****

10 Division of Denominators ending with 9

We will now have a look at one more specific case of division. Take the example of 1 / a9, where a = 1, 2, ——, 9. In the conversion of such fractions into recurring decimals, *Ekadhika (One more than Previous One)* process can be effectively used in division. Let's directly proceed to the example.

Example: Find the value of 1 / 19

First, we recognize the last digit of the denominator of the type 1 / a9. Here, the last digit is 9. For a fraction of the form, in whose denominator, 9 is the last digit, we take the case of 1 / 19 as follows:

For 1 / 19, 'previous' of 9 in 19 is 1. And one more than it, is 1 + 1 = 2.

Therefore 2 is the multiplier for the conversion. We write the last digit in the numerator as 1 and follow the steps leftwards.

Step 1 : 1

Step 2 : 21(multiply 1 by 2, put to left)

Step 3 : 421(multiply 2 by 2, put to left)

Step 4 : 8421(multiply 4 by 2, put to left)

Step 5 : 168421 (multiply 8 by 2 =16, 1 carried over, 6 put to left)

Step 6 : 1368421 (6 x 2 =12,+1 [carry over] = 13, 1 carried over, 3 put to left)

Step 7 : 7368421 (3 x 2, = 6 +1 [Carry over] = 7, put to left)

47

Step 8	:	147368421 (as in the same process)
Step 9	:	947368421 (Do – continue to step 18)
Step 10	:	18947368421
Step 11	:	178947368421
Step 12	:	1578947368421
Step 13	:	11578947368421
Step 14	:	31578947368421
Step 15	:	631578947368421
Step 16	:	12631578947368421
Step 17	:	52631578947368421
Step 18	:	1052631578947368421

Now, from step 18 onwards, the same numbers and order towards left will continue.

Thus, **1/19 = 0.052631578947368421**

It is interesting to note that we have

i) Not used division process at al

ii) Instead of dividing 1 by 19 continuously, we just multiplied 1 by 2 and continued to multiply the result successively by 2.

Exercise 8:

Find the decimal form for the problem using Denominator Ending in 9 (Ekadhika) method:

1) 1/9   2) 1/29   3) 1/59

****

11 General Method for Division

We saw many techniques for the Division of numbers involving specific cases like numbers ending with 9, series of 9, etc. Now, let us have a look at one general method which allows us to divide any number. This is achieved by the aphorism *"Transpose and Adjust"*.

The aphorism *"Transpose and Adjust"* is described by the *sutra "Paravartya Yojayet"*. Let us directly apply the *sutra* to our examples.

Example: Divide the following numbers: $1464 \div 12$.

Step 1 : (From left to right) Write the Divisor. Write digits of divisor leaving the first digit and using negative (-) sign and place them below the divisor as shown.

$$\begin{array}{c} \mathbf{1\,2} \\ \hline \mathbf{-2} \end{array}$$

Step 2 : Write down the dividend to the right. Set apart the last digit for the remainder.

i.e.
$$\begin{array}{c|cc} 1\,2 & 146 & 4 \\ -\,2 & & \end{array}$$

Step 3 : Write the 1st digit (1) below the horizontal line as it is.
Now, multiply this digit (1) by –2, write the product (-2) below the 2nd digit (4) and then add them.

Thus, we have 2nd digit of the answer as $(4 - 2) = 2$

i.e.

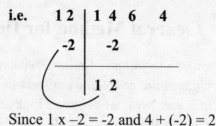

Since 1 x –2 = -2 and 4 + (-2) = 2

Step 4 : Repeating the same procedure, multiply 2 with -2, and write their answer (-4) under 6.

Do the same for next digit 2.

```
12  | 1  4  6  4
- 2 |   -2 -4
    |_____
    | 1  2  2  4
```

Step 5: Continue the process to the last digit.

i.e.

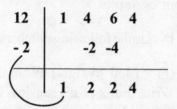

Step 6 : The sum of the last digit is the Remainder and the result to its left is the Quotient.

Thus, **Q = 122** and **R = 0**

Example : Divide the following numbers 1327 ÷ 13.

Following the steps in the above example, we get the following result:

```
13  | 1  3  2  7
-3  |   -3  0 -6
    |_____
    | 1  0  2  1    Q = 102, R = 1
```

Example: Divide following numbers 2598 ÷ 123.

Note that the divisor has 3 digits. So, we have to set up the last two digits of the dividend for the remainder.

1	2	3	25	98	Step (1) & Step (2)
	-2	-3			

Now proceed with the sequence of steps write –2 and –3 as follows:

1	2	3	2	5	9	8
	-2	-3		-4		-6
			↓		-2	-3
			2	1	1	5

Since   **2 x (-2, -3) = -4 , -6;**

And   **1 x (-2, -3) = -2, -3;**

9 – 6 – 2 = 1;

8 – 3 = 5.

Hence **Q = 21** and **R = 15.**

Example: Divide the following: 13456 ÷ 1123

1	1	2	3	1	3	4	5	6
	-1	-2	-3		-1	-2	-3	
				↓	-2	-4		-6
				1	2	0	-2	0

51

Note that the remainder portion contains –20, i.e. a negative quantity. To overcome this situation, take 1 over from the quotient column, i.e. 1123 over to the right side, subtract the remainder portion 20 to get the actual remainder.

Thus **Q = 12 – 1 = 11, and R = 1123 - 20 = 1103.**

Exercise 9:

Find the Quotient and Remainder for the problems using Transpose and Adjust (Paravartya Yojayet) method:

1) 472 ÷ 12

2) 3202 ÷ 11

3) 4594 ÷ 14

****

12   Squaring of numbers ending with 5

Having looked at various techniques to multiply and divide numbers, we now look at the unique technique that Vedic Mathematics has provided us to find the Squares of the numbers. We will use the aphorism "One more than Previous One" to find the square of numbers.

The aphorism *"By One more than the Previous One"* is described by the *sutra* *"Ekadhikena Purvena."* One of the most important applications of this *sutra* is 'squaring of numbers ending with 5.

Consider the following example:

Example: Obtain the **square** of number **45**.

$$45^2 = ?$$

Following are the steps to obtain the square of 45:

Step 1 :   Divide the answer into 2 parts.

$$45^2 = \boxed{\big|}$$

Step 2 :   For the number 45, the last digit is 5 and the 'previous' digit is 4. Take the square of last digit, i.e., 5^2 which is 25, and write it in the second part.

$$45^2 = \boxed{\big|\ 25\ }$$

Step 3 :   To fill the first part, use the formula:

$$n\,(n + 1)$$

where '**n**' is the first digit.

53

Step 4 : Here, we use **'one more than the previous one'** formula. The first digit i.e. **'n'** over here is **4**. So, keep **4** in place of **'n'** in above formula.

i.e.   we get: $4(4+1)$
$$= 4 \times 5$$
$$= 20$$

Step 5 : Thus put 20 in first part:

$45^2 =$ | 20 | 25 |

Thus, $45^2 = 2025$.

In the same way, consider another example.

Example: Obtain the **square** of **95**.

$95^2 = ?$ [ ]

Step 1 : Divide the answer into 2 parts.

$95^2 =$ [|]

Step 2 : For the number 95, the last digit is 5 and the 'previous' digit is 9. Take the square of last digit, i.e. 5^2 which is 25, and write it in the second part.

$95^2 =$ [| 25]

Step 3: To fill the first part, use the formula:

$n(n+1)$

where **'n'** is the first digit.

Step 4 : Hence, we use 'one more than the previous one' formula. The first digit i.e. 'n' over here is **9**. So, keep **9** in place of 'n' in above formula.

i.e., we get: **9 (9 + 1)**

$$= 9 \times 10$$

$$= 90$$

Step 5 : Put 90 in first part:

$$95^2 = \boxed{\begin{array}{c|c} 90 & 25 \end{array}}$$

Thus, 95^2 = 9025.

Similarly, we can get squares of:

105^2 = 10 x 11 | 25 = 11025;

135^2 = 13 x 14 | 25 = 18225;

Exercise 10:

Find the Squares of following using 'By One more than the Previous One' *(Ekadhikena Purvena)* process:

1) 75

2) 155

3) 995

****

13   Squaring a number by *Duplex Method*

We have already learnt a method useful to find the square of a number. But that method is useful under certain situations and conditions only. Now, we go through a more general formula.

The *sutra **Dwandwa-yoga (Duplex combination process)*** is used in two different ways. They are

i) By squaring

ii) By cross-multiplying.

We will use the *sutra **Dwandwa-yoga*** to find the square of the numbers.

Duplex :   We denote the Duplex of a number by the symbol D. We define for a single digit 'a', $D = a^2$.

And for a two digit number of the form 'ab', $D = 2 (a \times b)$.

If it is a 3 digit number like 'abc', $D = 2(a \times c) + b^2$.

For a 4 digit number 'abcd', $D = 2 (a \times d) + 2 (b \times c)$ and so on i.e. if the digit is single central digit, D represents 'square': and for the case of an even number of digits equidistant from the two ends, D represent the double of the cross- product.

Consider the examples:

Number	Duplex - D
3	$3^2 = 9$
6	$6^2 = 36$
23	$2(2 \times 3) = 12$
64	$2(6 \times 4) = 48$
128	$2(1 \times 8) + 2^2 = 16 + 4 = 20$
305	$2(3\ 0 \times 5) + 0^2 = 30 + 0 = 30$
4231	$2(4 \times 1) + 2(2 \times 3)$ $= 8 + 12$ $= 20$

Further, observe that for a n-digit number, the square of the number contains 2n or 2n-1 digits. Thus in this process, we take extra dots to the left one less than the number of digits in the given numbers.

Example: Find 62^2

Since number of digits = 2, we take one extra dot to the left.

$$
\begin{array}{ll}
.62 & \text{for } 2, D = 2^2 = 4 \\
644 & \text{for } 62, D = 2 \times 6 \times 2 = 24 \\
\textit{Carry} \quad \overline{\;32\;} & \text{for } 062, D = 2(0 \times 2) + 6^2 \\
& \qquad\qquad = 36 \\
\overline{3844} &
\end{array}
$$

$\therefore 62^2 = \textbf{3844.}$

Step 1 : For a 2-digit number, we keep a single dot in front of the number.

Step 2 : Then, we individually find Duplex for each digit, first for units place, i.e. 2. Duplex (2) = 2^2 = 4.

Step 3 : Then, tens place and units place together, i.e. 62. Duplex (62) = 2 (6 x 2) = 24. Write 4 in the answer and carry *2*.

Step 4 : Then, we assume dot to be 0 and calculate duplex for entire three digit number 062.

Duplex (062) = 2 (0 x 2) + 6^2 = 36.
Answer = 36.
Write 6 in the answer and carry 3.

Step 5 : Add carry 3 with 0 = 3.
Final Answer = **3844**.

Example: Find 234^2

Number of digits = 3. Extra dots =2
Following the above steps, we can solve this problem as follows:

..234   for 4, D = 4^2 = 16

42546   for 34, D = 2 x 3 x 4 = 24

Carry →   *1221*   for 234, D = 2 x 2 x 4 + 3^2 = 25

54756

for .234, D = 2x0x4 + 2x2x3 = **12**

for ..234, D = 2x0x4 + 2x0x3 + 2^2 = **4**

Step 1 : For a 3-digit number, we put two dots in front of the number.

Step 2 : Then, we individually find Duplex for each digit, first for units place, i.e. 4. Duplex $(4) = 4^2 = 16$. Write 6 and 1 is carry over.

Step 3 : Then, tens place and units place together, i.e. 34. Duplex $(34) = 2 (3 \times 4) = 24$.

Write 4 in the answer and carry 2.

Step 4 : Then, hundreds place, tens place and units place together, i.e. 234.

Duplex $(234) = 2 (2 \times 4) + 3^2 = 25$.
Write 5 in the answer and carry 2.

Step 5 : Then, we assume the first dot to be 0 and calculate duplex for four digit number 0234.

Duplex $(0234) = 2(0 \times 4) + 2(2 \times 3) = 12$

Answer = 2 and carry 1.

Step 6 : Then, we assume the second dot to be 0 and calculate duplex for entire 5 digit number 00234.

Duplex $(00234) =$

$$2(0 \times 4)$$
$$+ \quad 2(0 \times 3)$$
$$+ \quad 2^2$$
$$= \quad 4$$

Answer = 4 and carry 0.

Step 7 : Thus, adding the carry over digits, the answer comes to : **54756**

Example: 1426^2.

Number of digits = 4, extra dots = 3

Following the above steps, we can solve this problem as follows:

	...1426	6, D = 36
	1808246	26, D = 2x2x6 = 24
Carry →	22523	426, D = 2x4x6 + 2² = 52

2033476

1426, D = 2x1x6 + 2x4x2 = 28

.1426, D = 2x0x6 + 2x1x2 + 4²=20

..1426, D = 2x0x6 + 2x0x2 + 2x1x4 = 8

...1426, D = 1² = 1

Thus, 1426^2 = **2033476.**

With a little bit of practice, the results can be obtained mentally as a single line answer.

Exercise 11:

Find the Squares of following numbers using 'Duplex Combination Process' *(Dwandwa Yoga)* process:

1) **47**

2) **111**

3) **2043**

60   ********

14 Finding the Cube of a number by *"Extent of Deficiency"* Method

Vedic Mathematics provides two unique techniques for obtaining the cube of a number that requires less time and gives higher efficiency.

They are:

(i) Extent of Deficiency (*Yaavadunam*)

(ii) Ratio Method.

We will discuss the first technique in this chapter. The aphorism *"Extent of Deficiency"* is described by the *sutra "Yaavadunam"*. *Yaavadunam* is the tenth <u>sutra</u> of <u>Vedic Mathematics</u>. The *sutra* is used to find the cube of numbers.

Cubing the numbers that are near the power of 10, such as 13, 104, 1012, etc.:

Example: Find 12^3

Step 1   :   Subtract the nearest power of ten from the number: $12 - 10 = 2$

Step 2   :   Double this number and add the number being cubed: $(2 \times 2) + 12 = \mathbf{16}$

Step 3   :   Subtract from this number the power of ten as in step 1: $16 - 10 = 6$

Step 4   :   Multiply this number by the answer in step 1 : $2 \times 6 = \mathbf{12}$

Step 5:   Cube the answer in step 1: $2^3 = \mathbf{8}$

Step 6 : Since, we're cubing a 2 digit number, add two zeros to the answer in step 2 : 1600

Step 7 : Add 1 zero to the answer in step 4: 120

Step 8 : Add the answers in steps 7 and 6 to the answer in step 5: 1600 + 120 + 8 = 1728

Thus, **12^3 = 1728**

Cubing numbers that are near a <u>multiple</u> of a power of 10, such as 42, 507, 2008, etc.:

Here, it is important to understand 2 terms:

1.   Main Base: This number will always be a power of 10. For example, it can be 10, 100, 1000 and so on.

2.   Working Base: This number is the multiple of the power of 10. For example, if you are finding the cube of 52, your working base will be **50**, as it is nearest to the multiple of power of 10, i.e. 50.

Example: Find 48^3

Step 1 : Keep in mind that the *main base* is 10 and our *working base* will be 50

Step 2 : Divide the main base by the working base: 10 / 50 = 1/5

Step 3 : Subtract the working base from the number being cubed: 48-50= -2

Step 4 : Double this number and add the number being cubed: (-2 x 2) + 48 = 44

Step 5 : Divide this number by the square of the ratio found in *Step 2:* 44 / (1/5)² = 44 / (1/25) = 44 x 25 = **1100**

Step 6 : Subtract the working base from the answer in *Step 4:* 44 - 50 = -6

Step 7 : Multiply the answer in step three by the answer in *Step 6:* - 2 x -6 =12

Step 8 : Divide this number by the ratio in *Step 2:* 12 / (1/5) = 12 x 5 = **60**

Step 9 : Cube the answer found in *Step 3 :* $-2^3 = -8$

Step 10 : Since, we're cubing a 2 digit number, add two zeros to the answer in *Step 5:* 110000

Step 11 : Add 1 zero to the answer in *Step 8:* 600

Step 12 : Add the answers in *Steps 10 and 11* to the answer in *Step 9:* 110000 + 600 + -8 = 110592

Thus, $48^3 = 110592$

Exercise 12:

Find the Cubes of following numbers using 'Extent of Deficiency' *(Yaavadunam)* process:

1) 17

2) 52

3) 73

****

15 Finding the Cube of number by the *Ratio Method*

In this chapter, we will look at one more method to find the cubes of numbers. Let us take an example to understand this method.

Example: Find 14^3

The following are the steps to be followed to obtain the cube of 14:

Step 1 : Find the ratio of the two digits i.e.1:4

Step 2 : Now, write the cube of the first digit of the number i.e. 1^3

Step 3 : Now, write numbers in a row of 4 terms in such a way that the first one is the cube of the first digit and remaining three are obtained in a geometric progression with common ratio as the ratio of the original two digits (i.e. 1:4) Hence. the row is

1   4   16   64.

Step 4 : Write twice the values of 2nd and 3rd terms respectively under the terms in a second row as shown below:

i.e.   1   4   16   64
         8   32

($\because$ 2 x 4 = 8, 2 x 16 = 32)

Step 5 : Add the numbers column wise and follow carry over process.

1	4	16	64	Since $16 + 32 + 6$ (carryover) = 54
	8	32		4 written and 5 (carryover) + 4 + 8 = 17
2	7	4	4	7 written and 1 (carryover) + 1 = 2.

Thus, cube of 14 is **2744**.

Example: Find 18^3

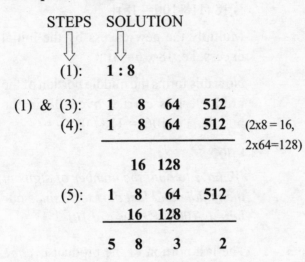

STEPS   SOLUTION

(1):   **1 : 8**

(1) & (3):   **1   8   64   512**

(4):   **1   8   64   512**   (2x8 = 16, 2x64=128)

16   128

(5):   **1   8   64   512**

16   128

5   8   3   2

Thus, $18^3 =$ **5832.**

Example: Find 33^3

STEPS   SOLUTION

(1):   **3 : 3**

(1) & (3):   **27   27   27   27** $(3^3=27)$

(4) & (5):   **27   27   27   27**   (2 x 27 = 54)

54   54

35   9   3   7

Thus, $33^3 =$ **35937**

Example: Consider 106^3.

Step 1 : The base is 100 and excess is 6.

     In this example, we **double the excess** and **then add to the number.**

     i.e. 106 + 12 = 118. (2 x 6 =12)

     This becomes the left - most portion of the cube. i.e. 106^3 = 118 / - - - -

Step 2 : Now, in the number 118, the new excess is 18 (118-100 = 18)

     Multiply the new excess by the initial excess. i.e. 18 x 6 = 108

     Now this forms the middle portion of the product. 1 is carried over, 08 in the middle. i.e. 106^3 = 118 / 08 / - - - - -

     Carry →   *1*

     We have to limit the number of digits in the middle and last part to 2, since our base is 100 (2nd power of 10)

Step 3 : The last portion of the product is **cube of the initial excess.** i.e. 6^3 = 216.

     16 in the last portion and 2 carried over.

     i.e. 106^3 = 118 / 08 / 16 = **1191016**

     Carry →   *1*   *2*

Example: Find 1002^3.

Step 1 : The base is 1000 and excess is 2.

     Since we **double the excess** and **then add**, the left- most portion of the cube becomes **1002 + (2 x 2) = 1006**

     i.e. 1002^3 = 1006 / - - - -

Step 2 : (New excess) x (initial excess)

     6   x   2   = 12

Thus, 012 forms the middle portion of the cube.

We need to have the number of digits in the middle and last part as 3, since our base is 1000 (3rd power of 10)

Step 3 : Cube of initial excess = 2^3 = 8. So, the last portion is 008.

We need to have the number of digits in the middle and last part as 3, since our base is 1000 (3rd power of 10)

Thus, 1002^3 =   1006 / 012 / 008

       =   **1006012008.**

Exercise 13 :

Find the Cubes of following numbers using 'Ratio Method' process:

   1) 19

   2) 103

   3) 4003

****

16 Validating the answers by *Beejank Method*

Apart from calculating the results at a faster rate, Vedic Mathematics also provides us with the method of validating our answers for correctness.

This can be achieved with the help of the *Beejank* method.

Beejank: The sum of the digits of any particular number is called the *Beejank*. If the addition is a two (or more) digit number, then this also can be added up to get a single digit.

E.g.   :   *Beejank* of 25 is 2 + 5 = 7.

Beejank of 448 is 4 + 4 + 8 = 16

Further, 1 + 6 = 7. i.e. 7 is a *Beejank*.

$$Beejank \text{ of } 1234 = 1 + 2 + 3 + 4$$
$$= 10$$
$$= 1$$

i.e. *Beejank* of 1234 is *1*.

Another method of finding *Beejank*:

Beejank is not at all affected if a number 9 is added to or subtracted from the number. This nature of number 9 helps in finding the *Beejank* very quickly, by cancelling 9 or the digits adding to 9 from the number.

Example: Find the *Beejank* of 254316.

As above, we have to follow:

$$254316 \quad = 2 + 5 + 4 + 3 + 1 + 6$$
$$= 21$$
$$= 2 + 1$$
$$= 3$$

But a quick look shows that numbers 5 & 4; 3 & 6 are to be ignored because 6+3=9, 4+5=9.

Hence, the remaining numbers, $2 + 1 = 3$ is the *Beejank* of 254316.

Example:

Beejank of 1293456 $\quad = 1 + 2 + 9 + 3 + 4 + 5 + 6$
$$= 30$$
$$= 3 + 0$$
$$= 3$$

But, we can cancel 9, 3 & 6, 4 & 5 because in each case, the sum is 9.

Hence, remaining 3 is the *Beejank*.

Validation/Check by Beejank method:

Gunita Samuccayah *sutra* helps us achieve the check by the *Beejank* method. Observe the following examples.

(i)   45 + 91

     Beejank of 45 is $4 + 5 = 9$

     and that of 91 is $9 + 1 = 10$ and $1 + 0 = 1$

     Now $9 + 1 = 10$ and $1 + 0 = 1$ is the *Beejank* of the sum of the two numbers

     Further, $45 + 91 = 136$.

     Its *Beejank* is $1 + 3 + 6 = 10$ and $1+0 = 1$

     Thus, we have checked the correctness.

(ii)   111 + 222.

Beejank of 111   =   1 + 1 + 1

=   3

and **Beejank** of 222   =   2 + 2 + 2

=   6

Sum of these **Beejanks** are 3 + 6 = **9**

Note that

111 + 222   = 333

Beejank of 333   = 3 + 3 + 3

= **9**

Thus, we have checked the correctness.

(iii)   459 - 68

Beejank of 459   = 4 + 5 + 9

= 18

= 1 + 8

= **9**

Beejank of 68   = 6 + 8

= 14

= **5**

Difference of **Beejanks** 9 - 5 = **4**,

Note that 459 - 68 = **391**

Beejank of 391   = 3 + 9 + 1

= 13

= 1 + 3

= **4**

Thus, verified.

(iv) 468 - 192

Beejank of 468 = 9

Beejank of 192 = 3

Difference of **Beejanks** = 9 − 3 = **6**

Now 468 − 192 = 276

Beejank of 276 = **6**

Thus, verified.

(v) 14 x 12 = 168

Multiplication of **Beejanks** of

14 and 12 is 5 x 3 = 15 → 1 + 5 → **6**

Beejank of 168
→ 1 + 6 + 8 → 15 → 1 + 5 → **6**

Thus, verified.

(vi) 341 x 15 = 5115

Beejank of 341 → 3 + 4 + 1 → 8

Beejank of 15 → 1 + 5 → 6

Product of the **Beejanks**
= 8 x 6 → 48 → 4 + 8 →12 → **3**

Beejank of 5115 → 5 + 1 + 1 + 5 → 12 → **3**

Thus, verified.

(vii) $31^2 = 961$

Beejank of 31 → 3 + 1 → 4

square of it $= 4^2$ → 16 → **7**

Beejank of result = 961 → 9 + 6 + 1 →
16 → 1 + 6 **7**

Thus, verified.

71

(viii) $987^2 = 974169$

> **Beejank** of $987 \rightarrow 9 + 8 + 7 \rightarrow 24 \rightarrow 2 + 4 \rightarrow 6$
> Square of it $= 6^2 = 36 \rightarrow 3 + 6 \rightarrow 9$
>
> **Beejank** of result 974169
> $\rightarrow 9 + 7 + 4 + 1 + 6 + 9 \rightarrow 3 + 6 \rightarrow 9$
>
> Thus, verified.

(ix) **Beejank in Division:**

Let P, D, Q and R be the dividend, the divisor, the quotient and the remainder respectively

Further the relationship between them is $P = (Q \times D) + R$

Example : $267 \div 6$

> We know that $267 = (44 \times 6) + 3$
>
> Now, the **Beejank** check.
>
> $267 \rightarrow 2 + 6 + 7 \rightarrow 6$
>
> $(44 \times 6) + 3 \rightarrow$ **Beejank** $\{[(4 + 4) \times 6] + 3\}$
>
> $\rightarrow (8) \times (6) + 3$
>
> $\rightarrow 51$
>
> $\rightarrow 6$
>
> Thus, verified.

Example: $9118 \div 527$

> $9118 = (17 \times 527) + 159$
>
> **Beejank** of $9118 \rightarrow 9 + 1 + 1 + 8 \rightarrow 1$

Beejank of $\{[17 \times 527] + 159\} \rightarrow (8) \times (5) + 6$

$\rightarrow 46$

$\rightarrow 10$

$\rightarrow 1$

72 Thus, verified.

Exercise 14:

Verify the results of the following operations by the *Beejank* method:

1) 99 x 12

2) 874 + 998

3) 45550 – 23009

4) 565 ÷ 5

****

17   Appendix: Terms & Operations

All the *sutras* of Vedic Mathematics were originally written in the *Sanskrit* language. So, various terms and operations used in the problem solving techniques are also in *Sanskrit*. This section describes various *Sanskrit* terms and operations in English, along with suitable examples.

I) Purak: Purak means 'complement'

        E.g.:   Purak of 5 is 5 ($\because 10-5 = 5$)

                Purak of 1 is 9 ($\because 10-1 = 9$)

                —

                Purak of 8 is 2 ($\because 10-8 = 2$)

II) Ekanyuna: Ekanyuna means 'one less'

        E.g.:   Ekanyuna of 5 is 4

                Ekanyuna of 1 is 0

                —

                Ekanyuna of 8 is 7

III) Ekadhika: Ekadhika means 'one more'

        E.g.:   Ekadhika of 0 is 1

                Ekadhika of 1 is 2

                —

                Ekadhika of 8 is 9

IV) Rekhank: Rekhank means 'a digit with a bar on its top'. In other words, it is a negative number.

E.g.: A bar on $\overline{3}$ (3), is called *rekhank* 3 or bar -3. We treat *purak* as a *Rekhank*.

E.g.: $\overline{7}$ is 3 and $\overline{3}$ is 7

In some instances, we write negative numbers also with a bar on the top of the numbers as

-9 can be shown as $\overline{9}$.

-56 can be shown as $\overline{56}$.

V) Addition and subtraction using Rekhank:

Adding a bar-digit i.e. *Rekhank* to a digit means the digit is subtracted.

E.g.: $5 + \overline{2} = 3, 5 + \overline{4} = 1$ and $3 + \overline{3} = 0$

Subtracting a bar - digit i.e. *Rekhank* from a digit means the digit is added.

E.g.: $5 - \overline{2} = 7, 5 - \overline{4} = 9$ and $3 - \overline{3} = 6$

VI) Multiplication and Division using Rekhank:

1. Product of two positive digits or two negative digits (*Rekhanks*)

   E.g.: $2 \times 4 = 8; \overline{5} \times \overline{3} = 15$
   i.e. always positive

2. Product of one positive digit and one *Rekhank*

   E.g.: $3 \times \overline{3} = \overline{9}$ or -9; $\overline{7} \times 3 = \overline{21}$ or -21
   i.e. always a *Rekhank* or negative.

3. Division of one positive by another or division of one *Rekhank* by another *Rekhank*.

   E.g.: $12 \div 2 = 6, \overline{12} \div \overline{3} = 4$
   i.e. always positive

4. Division of a positive by a *Rekhank* or vice versa.

      E.g.: $15 \div 5 = 3, 4 \div 2 = 2$

      i.e. always negative or *Rekhank*.

VII) Beejank: As we have already seen in the previous chapter, the sum of the digits of any particular number is called *Beejank*.

    E.g.: *Beejank* of 18 is $1 + 8 = 9$.

    Beejank of 847 is $8 + 6 + 2 = 16$

    Further, $1 + 6 = 7$. i.e. 7 is a *Beejank*.

$$\begin{aligned} \textit{Beejank of } 991 \; &= 9 + 9 + 1 \\ &= 1 + 9 \\ &= 1 + 0 \\ &= 1 \end{aligned}$$

  i.e., *Beejank* of 991 is *1*.

****

ANSWERS

Exercise 1:

    (A) 1) 72

           2) 27

           3) 12

    (B) 1) 25

           2) 40

           3) 21

Exercise 2:

    (A) 1) 8439

           2) 1236235

           3) 999975

    (B) 1) 8811

           2) 1110525

           3) 1089000

Exercise 3:

    (A) 1) 5742

           2) 426573

           3) 24817518

    (B) 1) 891

           2) 99900

           3) 19988001

Exercise 4:

   (A) 1) 275

        2) 847

        3) 1089

   (B) 1) 990

        2) 957

        3) 539

Exercise 5:

   (A) 1) 400

        2) 29318

        3) 179896

   (B) 1) 377

        2) 9506

        3) 48789

Exercise 6:

   (A) 1) $Q = 5, R = 7$

        2) $Q = 37, R = 7$

        3) $Q = 690, R = 0$

   (B) 1) $Q = 4, R = 3$

        2) $Q = 26, R = 7$

        3) $Q = 634, R = 6$

Exercise 7:

        1) 0.12500000000000...

        2) 0.20000000000000...

        3) 0.11111111111111...

Exercise 8 :

    1) 0.1111111111111...

    2) 0.03448275862068965517240379 31

    3) 0.01694915254237288135593220 3389831

Exercise 9 :

    1) Q = 39, R = 4

    2) Q = 291, R = 1

    3) Q = 328, R = 2

Exercise 10:

    1) 5625   2) 24025   3) 990025

Exercise 11 :

    1) 2209   2) 12321   3) 4173849

Exercise 12:

    1) 4913   2) 140608   3) 389017

Exercise 13:

    1) 6859

    2) 1092727

    3) 64144108027

Exercise 14:

    1) 1188   2) 1872

    3) 22541   4) 113

****

Author's Profile

Himanshu Pancholi is a Bachelor of Engineering in Information Technology. He graduated from Sardar Patel University, Mumbai. At present, he is working as a Senior Software Engineer with a MNC in Cyprus (Europe).

The author has previously written a couple of books on the same subject of Vedic Mathematics. This book covers even new techniques, which were not a part of the previous books. The author's keen interest in numbers led him to seek this topic. For the same reason, our readers will definitely see more titles in the future related to numbers, from the Author.

Apart from these books on Vedic Mathematics, Himanshu Pancholi has also published several White-papers on the subjects of Project Management and Employee Attitude. In time to come, readers can enjoy a few more books from him on the subjects such as Mysterious Numbers and Unexplained Techniques of Management.